Brother 2 Brother:
365 In/365 Out
Daily Motivational Quotes

Written by EL

Copyright © 2023 B.A.G. LLC

ISBN 979-8-218-21702-0

All rights reserved. No portion of the book may be reproduced or utilized in any form or by any means, electronic or mechanical, including photocopying, recording, or by any other information storage and retrieval system, without permission in writing from the author.

DISCLAIMER: The material in this book may include information by third parties. Third-party quotes are comprised of the opinions expressed by their owners. As such, the author of this book does not assume responsibility for any third–party quotes.

The publishing of such third–party quotes does not constitute the author's guarantee of any information or instruction contained. within the third–party quotes. Publication of such third–party quotes is simply an expression of the author's own opinion of that material.

THANK YOU
___

#TMN1, thank you for helping bring this vision to life. Uncle Rodney, I pray you are resting peacefully. Please continue to watch over us all.

Special thank you to everyone who supports my B2B brand and series!

Books:

Book 1: *Brother 2 Brother: Motivational Quotes and Lessons Learned*

Book 2: *Brother 2 Brother: 365 In/365 Out Daily Motivational Quotes*

Journals:

Book 3: *Brother 2 Brother: Journey to Healing Journal*

Book 4: *From Darkness to Light: Empowering Teen Boys with Incarcerated Fathers Journal*

Book 5: *From Darkness to Light: Empowering Teen Girls with Incarcerated Fathers Journal*

Activity Books:

Book 6: *Brother 2 Brother: Inmate Activity Book*

Book 7: *Brother 2 Brother: Keeping Your Mind Stimulated Activity Book*

Please continue to support. Everything is on Amazon!

FOREWORD

BY

MARCUS RANDLE EL, JR.

Yo, what's up fellas?

I gotta give it to you straight, no sugarcoating. Life ain't always a smooth ride. We all face obstacles, setbacks, and moments that knock us down. But the truth is: You got the power to rise up, shake off the dirt, and come out stronger than ever. Being the son, I overcame challenges. In my past, I've been depressed and had suicidal thoughts. When I was in that dark place, I used objects to cut my arm to help me with the pain. I'm telling you this because I believe that if you are going through something similar or even worse, this book would hit the heart. I'm healed from a lot of things that I never discussed with my parents or others. I continue to heal as a man as I experience life and my perspective on things have shifted as I grow into manhood.

This right here is more than just another book. It's a RAW, REAL & RELATABLE to help you understand the journey of manhood. It's diving into the nitty-gritty, straight, no chaser because that's how life is. It's time to unleash the beast within, tap into your untapped potential, and make your dreams a reality. Look, no need to dwell on past mistakes or be down about things out of your control. Nah, that's not how you operate. This is about taking charge of your life, standing tall, and steering it in the direction you want. It's about embracing your mistakes, leveraging your strengths, and creating a legacy that'll be remembered long after you're gone. I know what you're thinking: "But man, it's easier said than done." I hear you, Bro. Life throws curveballs, and sometimes it feels like you're swinging in the dark. But let me tell you, the darkest nights breed the brightest stars. Once you take that blindfold off you will see other doors open up that you didn't know was there.

It's in those moments of struggle that your true character is revealed. See, life ain't always a smooth ride, and we all go through our share of struggles. But guess what? We ain't gonna let that define us. We're kings in the making, warriors in the battlefield of life, and this book is here to help us unleash our true potential. Now, you might be wondering, "Why should I listen to this dude?" Well, let me tell you why. My father, the author of this book, has been in the trenches, walked through the fire, and come out stronger despite injustices.. He's faced setbacks, heartbreaks, and moments of doubt, just like you. But he's found a way to rise above it all, and he's here to share those lessons with you.

To be completely honest, me and my dad didn't have the best relationship. However, I do have his characteristics and those got me where I am today. I'm grateful for that. I'm in the military, doing things I never in my life thought I would be doing. I'm in a whole different country writing this as we speak. Be mindful, I am the oldest of 7 between my mom and dad and I'm only 20. I'm turning 21 on June 9th. I'm a young black man that's married with a house and car. I'm not trying to tear y'all down. I'm telling you, you can change your life around like I did. Shine in a career field that you're comfortable in. Shine bright for you, your family, and future generation.

In these pages, he's gonna dive deep into the complexes of manhood. He'll tackle the tough stuff—the hustle, the grind, the relationships, and the self-improvement game. But hey, it won't be all serious business. He'll sprinkle some humor and real talk throughout, cause life's too short to be all doom and gloom. This ain't no fluffy, cookie-cutter self-help motivational book, bro. Nah, he's gonna keep it a buck fifty. He'll break down the barriers that hold us back, smash through the walls of self-doubt, and embrace the untapped potential within us. Remember, you're not alone in this journey. We're in it together. So buckle up, get your game face on, and let's take on life like the kings we were born to be. This book is your secret weapon, your roadmap to on how to push through 365 days, and your source of inspiration when the going gets tough.

Let's rise, fellas, and conquer the world!

CONTENTS

January: Month of Self-Examination, Dreams, & Discernment 9

February: Month of Believing in Yourself & Trusting the Process 40

March: Month of Healing, Redemption, & Strength 69

April: Month of Understanding Life, Adjusting & What Comes with It 101

May: Month of Growth & Lessons Learned 132

June: Month of Grindin', Focus, & Staying Disciplined 164

July: Month of Pushing Through, Fatherhood, & Relationships 195

August: Month of Mental Adjustments, Determination, & Self-Care 227

September : Month of Strengths & Resilience 259

October: Month of No Turning Back & Pushing Through 290

November: Month of Realizing Your Power & Greatness 322

December: Month of Reflection & Redirection 352

January: Month of Self-Examination, Dreams, & Discernment
_____

Day 1 of 365: January 1st

Chase knowledge, stack wisdom: Education ain't just about textbooks and classrooms. Seek knowledge from every corner, whether it's from OGs, mentors, or the streets themselves. Stay hungry to learn and stack that wisdom like a boss.

Day 2 of 365: January 2nd

You got dreams, right? Well, dreams don't work unless you do. So put in that work and watch your dreams turn into reality.

Day 3 of 365: January 3rd

Stay grinding, no time for slacking. Success ain't waiting, it's for the taking.

Day 4 of 365: January 4th

No matter where you're from, chase dreams like a boss. Get that money, flip the script, and never take a loss.

Day 5 of 365: January 5th

Use your discernment. Being at the wrong place, at the wrong time, with the wrong people can legit ruin your life.

Day 6 of 365: January 6th

Respect the game, young homie. Whatever your passion is, be it music, art, sports, or entrepreneurship, immerse yourself in it. Study the greats who came before you, learn from their journeys, and then add your own flavor to the mix. Leave your mark.

Day 7 of 365: January 7th

You are not defined by your circumstances; you are defined by how you rise above them.

Day 8 of 365: January 8th

Being a discerning man means you're not afraid to challenge the status quo. You question, you analyze, and you make decisions based on what's real.

Day 9 of 365: January 9th

Hard times don't define you, they refine you.

Hustle hard, and watch your dreams come true.

Day 10 of 365: January 10th

The road to success is always under construction. Embrace the detours, learn from the challenges, and keep moving forward.

Day 11 of 365: January 11th

Stay true to yourself, because ain't nobody gonna do you like you do!

Day 12 of 365: January 12th

Listen up, discernment is your GPS in life. It helps you navigate through the bull and make those wise moves that elevate you as a man.

Day 13 of 365: January 13th

Don't let the streets define you; define the streets. Your environment doesn't determine your destiny; it's your choices and determination that shape your future.

Day 14 of 365: January 14th

In a world full of doubters, be your own biggest believer. No one can stop you if you believe in yourself and put in the work. Stay focused, stay hungry.

Day 15 of 365: January 15th

Life's a marathon, not a sprint. Pace yourself, set goals, and stay committed. You might stumble, but remember, it's how you bounce back that defines you.

Day 16 of 365: January 16th

Grind hard, shine harder: Success doesn't come easy, but that's what makes the journey worth it. Put in the work, hustle with passion, and stay grounded in pursuing your dreams. The grind molds champions.

Day 17 of 365: January 17th

Loyalty is everything: Surround yourself with genuine people who got your back through thick and thin. Loyalty breeds success and builds solid foundations. Stay loyal to your homies, your woman, your family, and most importantly, yourself.

Day 18 of 365: January 18th

Take your time, young man. There are many lessons hidden in the work.

Day 19 of 365: January 19th

Embrace the struggle, embrace the hustle: The struggle is real, but it's what molds us into kings. Embrace the challenges, the late nights, and the sacrifices. Your hustle today will shape your empire tomorrow.

Day 20 of 365: January 20th

Lift others as you rise: Remember, a true king uplifts his people. As you climb the ladder of success, reach back and bring others up with you. Empower your community and make a positive impact wherever you go.

Day 21 of 365: January 21st

Being a man with discernment means you ain't just going with the flow. You're carving your own path, making choices that align with who you truly are.

Day 22 of 365: January 22nd

Stay focused, homie. Keep your eyes on the prize and don't let distractions throw you off track. Life will try to knock you down, but remember, you're a King and you got this.

Day 23 of 365: January 23rd

Stay true to yourself, bro. In a world that tries to mold you into something you're not, be unapologetically you. Embrace your uniqueness and let your authenticity shine. Your voice and perspective matter.

Day 24 of 365: January 24th

Listen up, kings, discernment is your superpower. It's what sets you apart, helping you see the truth when others are blinded by illusions.

Day 25 of 365: January 25th

Life ain't always gonna be smooth sailing, bro. You'll face setbacks and obstacles that make you question everything. But here's the secret sauce: bounce back stronger every time. Embrace resilience, and let it be your superpower. It's not about how many times you fall; it's about how many times you get up.

Day 26 of 365: January 26th

Remember, you have the power to shape your destiny. Believe in yourself, put in the work, and keep your eyes on the prize. The world is yours for the taking. Now go out there and make it happen!

Day 27 of 365: January 27th

Life's gonna throw you curveballs, no doubt. But remember, it's not about how hard you fall; it's about how you rise back up. Use every setback as fuel to push yourself even harder. Embrace challenges as opportunities for growth.

Day 28 of 365: January 28th

Stay hungry, stay humble. Never lose that hunger for success, but don't let it cloud your judgment. Stay humble and grounded along the way. Remember where you came from and appreciate the journey. Arrogance won't take you far, but humility will earn you respect.

Day 29 of 365: January 29th

So, young kings, go out there, work hard, and remember these words. Let your journey be a testament to your determination, resilience, and undeniable greatness. Keep pushing, and never stop grinding!

Day 30 of 365: January 30th

Stay hungry, stay humble. Never lose sight of who you are and where you come from. Your roots give you strength, but your dreams give you wings. So spread them wide and soar high.

February: Month of Believing in Yourself & Trusting the Process

_____

Day 31 of 365: February 1ˢᵗ

Embrace Failure, Learn, and Bounce Back. Read that as many times as you need to until it sync in.

Day 32 of 365: February 2nd

Despite your confidence, you are about to discover that you are not fully in control and every choice comes with a chance to either get it right or get it wrong.

Day 33 of 365: February 3rd

Sometimes deciding who you are is deciding who you will never be again.

Day 34 of 365: February 4th

Success starts with the right mindset. Stay positive, believe in yourself, and don't let anyone hold you back. Surround yourself with people who uplift you and push you to be the best version of yourself.

Day 35 of 365: February 5th

Believe in yourself. Confidence is key. Trust in your abilities and believe that you can achieve greatness. The journey might get tough, but with self-belief, you'll overcome any obstacle that comes your way.

Day 36 of 365: February 6th

Don't be afraid of failure; be afraid of not trying. Every great achievement starts with a leap of faith.

Day 37 of 365: February 7th

Know that it's okay to ask for help along the way.

None of us make it alone.

Day 38 of 365: February 8th

Own your story, flip the script." Your past doesn't define you, homie. We all got a story, and it's up to you to own it. No matter where you've been, you can always flip the script and create a future that's entirely your own.

Day 39 of 365: February 9th

Stay woke, stay hungry." Don't let complacency or ignorance hold you back. Stay woke to what's happening in the world around you, stay hungry for knowledge and growth. The hunger for success should never fade.

Day 40 of 365: February 10th

Rise above the noise, be your own voice. In a world filled with noise and distractions, it's important to find your own voice and let it be heard.

Day 41 of 365: February 11th

Remember, young kings, you got greatness within you. Don't let anyone tell you otherwise.

Day 42 of 365: February 12th

Bounce back from setbacks, learn from your mistakes, and keep pushing forward. Your strength lies in your ability to rise above adversity and come out even stronger.

Day 43 of 365: February 13th

Lead by example, homie. Inspire others with your actions, your words, and your integrity. Show the world that you can achieve greatness while staying true to your roots. Be the role model you wish you had growing up.

Day 44 of 365: February 14th

Embrace your dreams, chase them with passion, Work hard, stay focused, ain't no time for slacking. Keep grinding, stay hungry, never lose sight, Success comes to those who hustle day and night.

Day 45 of 365: February 15th

In these streets, life can be tough, no doubt, But it's your individuality that will help you stand out. Speak your truth, express your voice with pride, Let your words and actions be your guide. Stay true to yourself, don't be afraid to be real, authenticity's the sauce that'll seal the deal. Be a leader, a role model for your crew, Inspire others with what you say and do.

Day 46 of 365: February 16th

Your'Are always one decision away from a totally different life. If nothing else. Remember that. You get a chance to make a choice. That choice can make or break you.

Day 47 of 365: February 17th

As men, we often pick up more than we need to carry. You don't have to hold onto everything that you pick up. Let go, it's cool.

Day 48 of 365: February 18th

A hater will try to discourage you with how hard something is that they never even tried. Keep your eyes on the prize.

Day 49 of 365: February 19th

Embrace the struggle, it's where you grow. Your past doesn't define you, it's the story you'll outgrow.

Day 50 of 365: February 20th

Real talk, you really gotta take the time to learn yourself, understand your triggers, realize your weak areas and change the way you think about a lot of sh*t. It ain't easy, but it'll save you from a lot of unnecessary drama.

Day 51 of 365: February 21st

Life is a journey with ups and downs. Embrace the struggles, for they mold you into a stronger version of yourself. And when you start to see those wins, no matter how small, celebrate them. You deserve to acknowledge your progress and give yourself props, my man.

Day 52 of 365: February 22nd

But yo, it's not just about your personal success. Lift your homies up along the way.

Day 53 of 365: February 23rd

Listen up, homie: Life's testin' you right now, but you're tougher than you realize. Rise up, show 'em what you're made of. You going to fight or are you going to fold?

Day 54 of 365: February 24th

Yo, keep your head up, fam. The struggle might be real, but so is your hustle. Keep grinding and watch how you shine in the end. Hard work pays off.

Day 55 of 365: February 25th

Bror, I see you going through some tough times, but know that strength ain't about never falling down, it's about getting back up every single time. Release the beast in you and get up stronger and go harder.

Day 56 of 365: February 26th

I know life's tryna bring you down, but you got that inner strength to rise above it all. Aye, you a lot stronger than you even know bro, real talk.

Day 57 of 365: February 27th

Don't be afraid to dream big and chase those dreams with everything you've got. Believe in yourself, trust your instincts, and know that you have the power to make those dreams a reality. Keep pushing forward and let nothing stand in your way!

Day 58 of 365: February 28th

You've got the power within you to overcome any obstacle that comes your way. Stay focused, stay hungry, and stay on your grind.

March: Month of Healing, Redemption, & Strength

_____

Day 59 of 365: March 1ˢᵗ

There is no way to prepare for losing loved ones; just understand that it will happen. Honor them by being grateful for each breath while they are living.

Day 60 of 365: March 2nd

Healing ain't about frontin' or fakin', it's about facing your demons and reclaiming your power.

Day 61 of 365: March 3rd

They say time heals all wounds, but to keep it real, it takes strength, patience, and a whole lot of forgiveness to stitch your heart back together.

Day 62 of 365: March 4th

Continue being patient in making moves and accepting that people will disappoint you. Everyone will not have the same love and loyalty as you.

Day 63 of 365: March 5th

Healing begins when we acknowledge your wounds and embrace the strength it takes to mend them.

Day 64 of 365: March 6th

Healing is a process, not a destination. Take it one step at a time."

Day 65 of 365: 7th

Sometimes you gotta lose yourself in the chaos to find the peace that heals.

Day 66 of 365: March 8th

To heal is to reclaim your power, to rise above your scars, and to become the embodiment of your own redemption.

Day 67 of 365: March 9th

A man who embraces his healing journey becomes a inspiration of hope, motivating others to find their own path to wholeness.

Day 68 of 365: March 10th

You can't pour from an empty cup, so fill yourself up with self-care, self-love, and healing vibes.

Day 69 of 365: March 11th

Healing teaches a man the art of self-compassion, reminding him that he is worthy of love, care, and gentle restoration.

Day 70 of 365: March 12th

Through healing, you'll learn to redefine your strength as the ability to face harsh reality, accept support, and emerge with newfound resilience. Don't disrupt your healing journey.

Day 71 of 365: March 13th

Healing teaches us that strength is not measured by how much we can endure, but by our willingness to heal and nurture ourselves.

Day 72 of 365: March 14th

The journey of healing for a man is an opportunity to rewrite the narrative of his life, transforming pain into purpose and wounds into wisdom.

Day 73 of 365: March 15th

Healing is the hustle of self-care, the grind of letting go, and the not taking L's on finding your peace.

Day 74 of 365: March 16th

Through healing, a man learns that scars are not a mark of brokenness, but a symbol of his journey—a roadmap of his experiences and the resilience he carries within

Day 75 of 365: March 17th

Healing requires the courage to let go of what no longer serves us, to release the weight of past hurts, and to embrace the freedom that comes with inner peace.

Day 76 of 365: March 18th

Healing invites us to rewrite our stories, to reclaim our narrative from the hands of pain and transform it into a tale of resilience, strength, and triumph.

Day 77 of 365: March 19th

Life may throw obstacles, but you gotta stay strong. Resilience is key, it's what'll keep you going long. Stay true to yourself, let your voice be heard. Don't let anyone tell you what you can and cannot achieve in this world.

Day 78 of 365: March 20th

Healing is a testament to the power. Not weighing on the things that hurt you or letting them shape your present experiences.

Day 79 of 365: March 21st

Level up, elevate your mind. Break through barriers, leave the non sense all behind.

Day 80 of 365: March 22nd

You are stronger than you think. Depression can make you feel weak and powerless, but remember that reaching out for help and acknowledging your struggles takes immense strength. You're already on the path to healing.

Day 81 of 365: March 23rd

The streets may be tough, but so are you. Rise up and claim your destiny.

Day 82 of 365: March 24th

You're not heartless, that's pain talking. You hate that fact that you love hard and the love you've shown people has been mishandled and misunderstood so much in your past.

Day 83 of 365: March 25th

How do you pick yourself up again? With confidence. With Intention. Apply lessons learned and don't repeat the same mistakes. Learn from your experience and don't allow anyone use your past against you.

Day 84 of 365: March 26th

Sometimes you have to make a decision that will hurt your heart but heal your soul. Life is just funny like that.

Day 85 of 365: March 27th

Don't let nobody box you in. You have a right to rewrite your story. Certain people will try to take you back to the man you used to be, never give them the satisfaction.

Day 86 of 365: March 28th

Sometimes God will take you from where you thought you needed to be to a place you don't want to see so you can finally grow into the man you were called to be. No cap.

Day 87 of 365: March 29th

You have to face the reality that you can be sorry for some of your past decisions, and people won't be ready to forgive you. That's life. Everybody heal on their on time and that's facts.

Day 88 of 365: March 30th

At your absolute BEST you still wont be good enough for the wrong woman. At your worst, you will still be WORTH it the right way woman. Remember this always.

Day 89 of 365: March 31st

Shout out to all the men that been hit back-to-back with the BS that comes with life but still pushing through. That's what real men do.

April: Month of Understanding Life, Adjusting & What Comes with It

---

Day 90 of 365: April 1st

Listen, you have to really make peace with the fact that people will hold different versions of you in their mind. Can't really dwell on that.

Day 91 of 365: April 2

Lack of self-control (chasing every woman you see), envy, greed, and all lower vibrational thoughts will keep you stuck. Avoid those things and always strive to be better.

Day 92 of 365: April 3

Trust yourself. Everything you want for yourself is yours to earn. You are already the version of yourself that you see in your head.

Day 93 of 365: April 4

You'll be older soon, and you'll learn more about yourself.

Day 94 of 365: April 5

Be mindful of what you consume. Everything in moderation is best. Too much of anything can be your biggest setback.

Day 95 of 365: April 6

Don't wait for the perfect moment; create it. Seize opportunities, take risks, and trust in your ability to navigate the unknown. A man that doesn't work, doesn't' eat.

Day 96 of 365: April 7

Success is not a destination but a journey. Embrace the process, learn from failures, and celebrate every step forward.

Day 97 of 365: April 8

Ain't no shortcuts to success, homie. Put in the work.

Day 98 of 365: April 9

In this game of life, be the player who turns obstacles into opportunities.

Day 99 of 365: April 10

It's all about the come up, so stay focused, stay hungry, and get that paper stacked up.

Day 100 of 365: April 11

The path to success is paved with doubters and naysayers. Use their negativity as your motivation to prove 'em wrong.

Day 101 of 365: April 12th

Embrace the struggle, 'cause that's where your strength is built.

Day 102 of 365: April 13th

Life's a mixtape, and you're the DJ. Drop the beats of determination, and make your dreams replay.

Day 103 of 365: April 14th

You got this, fam! Keep pushin' forward and show 'em what you're made of.

Day 104 of 365: April 15th

The world is yours bro, so step into it with confidence, purpose, and the belief that you can achieve anything you set your mind to. Keep hustlin', keep shining, and keep winning. You got this!

Day 105 of 365: April 16th

Elevate your mind, break the chains. Break free from any limitations or negative influences that hold you back. Expand your knowledge, seek wisdom, and strive for personal growth. Break the chains of doubt and reach for greatness.

Day 106 of 365: April 17th

Embrace the struggle, it builds your muscle. Life's challenges are stepping stones to your success. Embrace the struggles, learn from them, and let them strengthen your character. Remember, it's through adversity that you become the resilient man you're meant to be.

Day 107 of 365: April 18

Sometimes God takes you on a journey you didn't know you needed to bring you everything you wanted. Sometimes God will isolate you to save you.

Day 108 of 365: April 19

I'ma keep it real. Sometimes you win. Sometimes you learn.

Day 109 of 365: April 20

You made a choice to improve for a reason. NEVER circle back on habits or people that tried to break you. Stand on what you are working towards and stay disciplined.

Day 110 of 365: April 21

Sometimes the biggest fight is between you and your mind. That battle between a man's heart and his mind is a beast.

Day 111 of 365: April 22

Learn your triggers homie, so you know how to walk away when someone is trying you. If they see you give your power away with anger, they'll test you every single time & win.

Day 112 of 365: April 23

You just have to keep going and know that when it's all said and done, you're going to be okay. You've been given so many reasons to give up but you gotta push through the hardest times. No one is coming to save you. It'll be days where it's only you, your thoughts, and the Man above.

Day 113 of 365: April 24

Some people say there's always a blessing in disguise in every situation. I say there's always a lesson in disguise that comes from moments that test you the most.

Day 114 of 365: April 25

Just don't react at all. You don't need to. Not giving a toxic person the reaction that they're desperately seeking for is powerful.

Day 115 of 365: April 26

As a man, you have to get to a place where you're more self-aware and no longer repeating behaviors because you catch yourself before they even happen.

Day 116 of 365: April 27

The work it takes to understand all parts of you is hard, but it's worth it.

Day 117 of 365: April 28

You can't keep getting mad at people for playing in your face and you're the one giving them access to you. You gotta move like it's a privilege to know you and limit who has access to you.

Day 118 of 365: April 29

When in a relationship, you have to understand that you were both raised differently which means you may love differently, react differently, and communicate differently. The important part is that knowing that disagreements are okay, but disrespect is not.

Day 119 of 365: April 30

You can absolutely do it all. You can have it all. But how you get it, be careful. It'll be how you lose it.

May: Month of Growth & Lessons Learned

Day 120 of 365: May 1st

It ain't about where you come from, it's where you going. Don't let people pull you back into things you fought your way out of.

Day 121 of 365: May 2nd

No matter what happens, you can't lose. Finish the race you started and be proud of the race you run. Stand on that as a man.

Day 122 of 365: May 3rd

Hustle hard, don't let nobody play you. Keep pushing and prove 'em wrong, you'll be the one they look up to.

Day 123 of 365: May 4th

Obstacles are opportunities in disguise. Don't be afraid to face them head-on and keep going after what you want. Don't let sh*t get in your way.

Day 124 of 365: May 5th

Life's a battle, but you got the power. Rise above the struggles and own your hour.

Day 125 of 365: May 6th

Don't stress the small stuff, homie. Keep your eyes on the prize and let the petty stuff slide. It's not worth your freedom.

Day 126 of 365: May 7th

Remember, it's not just about the destination; it's about the journey. Each step you take, every setback you face, builds character and strength. Embrace the struggle, 'cause that's where growth happens.

Day 127 of 365: May 8th

Forgive the people that wasn't able to love you the way that you needed. Then you have to forgive yourself for looking for love in the wrong places and the decisions you made as a result. Take accountability for the parts of your life based on feelings when you didn't know better.

Day 128 of 365: May 9th

Fact: Settling will never feel right when you know you're meant for more. Everything goes wrong when you're in a place not meant for you, remember that and work on your exit strategy.

Day 129 of 365: May 10th

Focus on what you can control, or you'll lose yourself every time. You can't f*ck up anything that is truly meant for you. What's yours, can't be taken away.

Day 130 of 365: May 11th

Don't deny the signs, the vibes, and the energy you get from certain people. As a man, it's important that you learn not to ever go against yourself. If it doesn't feel right, it's not right.

Day 131 of 365: May 12th

Some women hold you down, and some women HOLD YOU DOWN. Know the difference.

Day 132 of 365: May 13th

Hardest pill to swallow, sometimes you may be difficult to handle. As men, we keep a lot bottled in. But if you meet a woman that's willing to stay committed to understanding how to love you and wanting the best for you, don't let sh*t like ego and pride ruin it.

Day 133 of 365: May 14th

Don't let anyone use your past to invalidate your current mindset and where you at. A lot of people will try to provoke the older version of you.

Day 134 of 365: May 15th

You're doing a lot better than you give yourself credit for, bro. You may not be where you want or have the bag that you want but keep going hard. You'll get there. Doing things the right way takes time. Trust the process so you don't have to live with regrets.

Day 135 of 365: May 16th

Trust your gut, you ain't tweaking bro.

Day 136 of 365: May 17th

To attract better, you have to become better. You can't be on the same sh*t and expect different results. Life don't work like that homie.

Day 137 of 365: May 18th

Don't be too hard on yourself. Life ain't easy. Sometimes it'll feel like you're doing the best you can and still not getting what you deserve. That's when you'll be tested the most. Don't be tempted to cut corners. Put in the work and it'll pay off, even on the hardest days.

Day 138 of 365: May 19th

Yo, I feel you, my dude. Life's been dealing you some rough cards, but remember, you ain't folding. Keep playing that hand 'til you come out on top.

Day 139 of 365: May 20th

Don't trip, homie. You might be down right now, but you're destined for greatness. Rise up, grind hard, and let your success be the ultimate revenge

Day 140 of 365: May 21

"Listen up, my G. Tough times don't define you; they refine you. Embrace the struggle, cause when you come out the other side, you'll be shining brighter than ever!

Day 141 of 365: May 22

The world needs more men like you. Stay true to yourself, chase your dreams, and never give up. Success is just around the corner, waiting for you to claim it. Go out there and make it happen.

Day 142 of 365: May 23

You ain't gotta prove nothing to nobody but yourself & God. Show 'em what you're made of and leave 'em speechless.

Day 143 of 365: May 24

Your worth as a man is not determined by your ability to suppress emotions, but by your capacity to express and process them.

Day 144 of 365: May 25

Remember that you are not alone. There is a vast network of individuals who stand with you, support you, and believe in your potential. Seek out mentors, role models, and mentors that uplift and inspire you.

Day 145 of 365: May 26

You may not know it, but you are a role model for future generations. Embrace this responsibility with pride and lead by example. Your actions have the power to inspire and shape the world. In inspire people who pretend not to see you.

Day 146 of 365: May 27

When you face obstacles, don't be discouraged. Instead, see them as opportunities for growth and learning. Keep pushing forward, even when it feels like the odds are against you. Remember that setbacks are temporary, and with determination and perseverance, you can achieve great things.

Day 147 of 365: May 28

Take a moment to reflect on your past accomplishments and the times when you've overcome difficult situations. Use those memories as a source of inspiration and remind yourself of your inner strength. Trust in your abilities and believe that you have what it takes to achieve your goals.

Day 148 of 365: May 29

A lot of your homies won't celebrate you until your wins feel "big" enough for them. Them ain't really your homies. Open your eyes.

Day 149 of 365: May 30

Keep hustlin' and stay focused, 'cause the world won't wait for you. Chase your dreams like a boss, and make 'em all come true.

Day 150 of 365: May 31

Ain't no shame in wanting to be better. Embrace that growth mindset and keep hustling' every day. Remember, progress comes one step at a time.

June: Month of Grindin', Focus, & Staying Disciplined

_____

Day 151 of 365: June 1st

Respect the hustle, respect the game. No matter what you're doing, give it your all. Whether you're chasing a career, pursuing your passions, or takin' care of your family, put that heart and soul into it. Respect the grind and watch it pay off.

Day 152 of 365: June 2nd

Remember that failure is not the end; it's an opportunity to learn, adapt, and come back stronger than ever before. Now you move with experience.

Day 153 of 365: June 3rd

First things first, take a step back and peep inside yourself. Reflect on your thoughts, actions, and beliefs. Understand what's driving you and what's holding you back. Self-awareness is key, bro.

Day 154 of 365: June 4th

Discipline is the daily commitment to do what needs to be done, even when you don't feel like doing it. When you're no longer motivated, that's when your discipline kicks in.

Day 155 of 365: June 5th

A disciplined man understands that success is not a matter of chance but a result of deliberate action.

Day 156 of 365: June 6th

Nobody ever tells you how hard it is to really discipline yourself. They just tell you it's necessary. But to really focus and work towards the man you see yourself being, it takes GRIND. No short cuts. You can try to fake it until you make it, but that will only get you so far. DISCIPLINE is KEY.

Day 157 of 365: June 7th

Discipline is the key that unlocks the doors to your dreams. Keep turning that key.

Day 158 of 365: June 8th

Stay focused on your grind, cause ain't nobody gonna hand you success on a silver platter.

Day 159 of 365: June 9th

Dream big, grind hard, and make those moves. You got this, fam.

Day 160 of 365: June 10th

Respect the hustle, respect the game. No matter what you're doin', give it your all. Whether you're chasing a career, pursuing your passions, or takin' care of your family, put that heart and soul into it. Respect the grind and watch it pay off.

Day 161 of 365: June 11th

Sometimes it can feel as if no one can see all that you do and all that you goo through. The strong get tired, but you still gotta push through. Truth is, no one is coming to save you.

Day 162 of 365: June 12th

Your journey matters. Your dreams, ambitions, and aspirations are worth pursuing. Don't let anyone tell you otherwise. Keep striving for success, stay true to who you are, and make your mark on this world. You got the skills, talent, and determination to make it happen.

Day 163 of 365: June 13th

Remember, it's okay to stumble sometimes. We all do. But what separates winners from the rest is the ability to bounce back stronger. So embrace those setbacks, learn from them, and keep moving forward. Your resilience is what defines you, my man.

Day 164 of 365: June 14th

You have the power to rewrite the narrative. Break free from stereotypes, challenge expectations, and create a legacy that inspires others.

Day 165 of 365: June 15th

When things get tough, remember how far you've come. Look back at all the challenges you've already overcome and use them as fuel to keep moving forward

Day 166 of 365: June 16th

Take a moment to reflect on your values and what truly matters to you. Align your actions with your core principles, and you'll find clarity in your path."

Day 167 of 365: June 17th

Finding your way is a personal journey, and there is no one-size-fits-all approach. Stay true to yourself, be open to new experiences, and trust that the path will unfold before you.

Day 168 of 365: June 18th

Setbacks are temporary. Even though it may feel like you're stuck in a cycle of defeat, it's important to remind yourself that circumstances can change. Keep an open mind and believe in your ability to push through.

Day 169 of 365: June 19th

Discipline is the difference between who you are and who you want to be. As a man, you must remember that.

Day 170 of 365: June 20th

Let's talk about those thoughts that be holding you down. It's time to question 'em. Are they helping you or just keeping you stuck? Dead the negative vibes and start rockin' that growth mindset. Believe in yourself and the possibilities that lie ahead.

Day 171 of 365: June 21ˢᵗ

You're on a mission to be the best version of yourself, and that's commendable. Don't allow anyone to block the man you are aiming become.

Day 172 of 365: June 22nd

Listen up, homie! The fact that you're striving for improvement shows you have the drive and ambition to make things happen. Don't be afraid to step out of your comfort zone and embrace growth. Keep pushing forward!"

Day 173 of 365: June 23rd

Keep your head up, stay focused, and never forget that you have the power to transform your life.

Day 174 of 365: June 24th

Learn to forgive yourself: It's easy to be hard on yourself when you make a mistake, but holding onto guilt and shame can hinder your progress.

Day 175 of 365: June 25th

Remember that making mistakes is a natural and necessary part of life. It's through mistakes that we gain valuable lessons and insights. Now if you constantly repeat them, now that's on you.

Day 176 of 365: June 26th

Build Solid Connections. Form genuine relationships based on loyalty, respect, and shared ambitions. Remember, your network is your net worth, so choose your circle wisely.

Day 177 of 365: June 27th

You gotta stay hungry, stay humble, and always remember that the struggle only makes you stronger.

Day 178 of 365: June 28th

Many successful men have achieved greatness because they learned from their mistakes. Instead of dwelling on past failures, channel your energy into thinking differently and taking calculated risks.

Day 179 of 365: June 29th

If your mistake have impacted others, as a man, you should offer an apology and make amends whenever possible. Recognize the impact of your actions, express remorse, and demonstrate a commitment to positive change. Remember that seeking forgiveness is a sign of strength and shows your willingness to grow, it doesn't make you weak.

Day 180 of 365: June 30th

Remember, you have the power to overcome any challenge that comes your way. Believe in yourself and your abilities, because you're capable of achieving great things. Even when things get difficult, don't lose sight of your goals and dreams. Keep pushing forward, one step at a time.

July: Month of Pushing Through, Fatherhood, & Relationships

Day 181 of 365: July 1st

Remember, fatherhood is a lifelong journey of learning, growth, and love. Embrace this role with dedication, and know that you have the ability to make a profound and positive impact on your kids' lives.

Day 182 of 365: July 2nd

All though we are taught not to have regrets, you will have them. But if you don't let your past dies, it won't let you live.

Day 183 of 365: July 3

Fatherhood will scare the hell out of you, and it will also make you the best man that you could possibly be. Life is temporary, but the legacy you leave behind for your kids is forever.

Day 184 of 365: July 4th

Don't spend as much time attempting to figure it all out, as much as you spend the time to truly be present through the experiences. Bro, trust, there will be many of them.

Day 185 of 365: July 5th

Stay committed to your vision, even when faced with doubts and setbacks. Your unwavering dedication will lead you to success.

Day 186 of 365: July 6th

Learn from past experiences: Reflect on past relationships to identify patterns and learn from them. Assess what worked well and what didn't. This self-reflection will help you grow and make more informed choices in future relationships..

Day 187 of 365: July 7th

Encourage open communication and emotional expression with your kids. Create a safe space where they feel comfortable sharing their thoughts, fears, and joys. Teach them that vulnerability is a strength and that their emotions matter.

Day 188 of 365: July 8th

In a world full of doubters, be your own biggest believer. Trust in your abilities, stay motivated, and make it happen, no matter what

Day 189 of 365: July 9th

Understand that fatherhood is a continuous learning experience. Be willing to adapt, grow, and learn alongside your kids.

Day 190 of 365: July 10th

Break the cycle of negative stereotypes: Challenge negative stereotypes by being an involved, loving, and responsible father. Demonstrate that black men can be caring, nurturing, and successful parents. Help break down stereotypes and contribute to positive representations of black fatherhood.

Day 191 of 365: July 11ᵗʰ

To the young kings, go out there, conquer your dreams, and make your mark on this world. The journey won't be easy, but you got that fire within you. Rise above, embrace your hustle, and show the world what you're capable of.

Day 192 of 365: July 12th

Be there for her during both successes and challenges. Practice empathy by trying to understand her perspective and providing emotional support when she needs it.

Day 193 of 365: July 13th

You're capable of rising above the feeling of defeat. Don't give up on yourself, and remember that with time and grind, you will find your way.

Day 194 of 365: July 14th

It is essential to have shared values and goals with your woman. Talk about your goals, plans, and what you envision for your future together. Aligning your visions creates a strong foundation for your relationship.

Day 195 of 365: July 15th

Take a step back and gain perspective. Sometimes, when we're in the midst of a difficult situation, it's easy to lose sight of the bigger picture. Take a moment to reflect.

Day 196 of 365: July 16th

Your past does not dictate your future. Regardless of what has happened in the past, you have the power to shape your future.

Day 197 of 365: July 17th

Each challenge you face provides valuable lessons that can shape you into a stronger, wiser man. Accept that.

Day 198 of 365: July 18th

Above all, love your kids unconditionally. Let them know that your love is unwavering, regardless of their successes, failures, or challenges. Be a source of comfort, encouragement, and stability in their lives.

Day 199 of 365: July 19th

Communication is key: Foster open and honest communication with your woman. Listen actively, seek understanding, and express your thoughts and feelings respectfully. Effective communication builds stronger bonds.

Day 200 of 365: July 20th

You are a valuable and important presence in your kid's lives. Your love, guidance, and support make a significant impact on their development and well-being.

Day 201 of 365: July 21th

Expressing appreciation for your woman and those efforts can go a long way in strengthening your bond. Regularly acknowledge and thank her for the things that she does that makes a positive impact on your relationship and you being a better man.

Day 202 of 365: July 22nd

You see, life's a hustle, a constant grind, but don't let the struggles ever cloud your mind. In this crazy world you gotta stay true, to your ambitions, your goals, and everything you pursue.

Day 203 of 365: July 23rd

Leave a lasting legacy of love and support for your kids to remember. Be present not only in their childhood but throughout their lives. Your impact as a father extends far beyond their early years, shaping the men and women they become.

Day 204 of 365: July 24th

Practice active listening when your woman speaks or expresses herself. Give them your full attention, maintain eye contact, and respond genuinely. Show interest and empathy in their thoughts, concerns, and experiences.

Day 205 of 365: July 25th

Embrace your role as a father with pride and responsibility. Your involvement and active participation in your kids' lives are so important.

Day 206 of 365: July 26th

Quality time and presence matter more than material possessions. Be more than a provider. Make a conscious effort to spend dedicated, time with your kids.

Day 207 of 365: July 27th

Be accountable and learn from mistakes. As a man, take responsibility for your actions and behavior. Acknowledge and apologize when you make mistakes, and be open to learning and growing from them. Commit to personal growth and continuous improvement.

Day 208 of 365: July 28th

Create a safe space where she feels comfortable expressing her feelings, concerns, and desires. Listen actively and empathetically, and communicate your own thoughts and emotions effectively.

Day 209 of 365: July 29th

Above all, remember that your presence and love make a significant difference in your kids' lives. Embrace the joys and challenges of fatherhood and cherish the precious moments you share with your kids.

Day 210 of 365: July 30th

When life knocks you down, get up, dust yourself off, and keep pushing. Failure is just a detour, not a dead-end. Embrace the lessons, learn from them, and keep moving forward.

Day 211 of 365: July 31st

Remember, relationships require effort, patience, and ongoing commitment from both you and your lady. Building a strong and healthy relationship is a journey that involves continuous learning, growth, and a strong foundation built on loyalty and respect.

August: Month of Mental Adjustments, Determination, & Self-Care

_____

Day 212 of 365: August 1st

Real strength ain't just about muscles. It's about resilience, character, and the ability to overcome any obstacle that life throws your way. Flex that mental muscle..

Day 213 of 365: August 2nd

But it ain't just about you, man. It's about others too. Take a sec to understand where they comin' from. Clarity is a game-changer.. Open your mind, listen up, and see things from different angles. It's all about expanding your thoughts and understanding everyone doesn't think the way you do.

Day 214 of 365: August 3rd

Education ain't a one-time thing, bro. It's a lifelong hustle. Stay hungry for knowledge. Seek out new ideas, soak up different viewpoints, and keep leveling up your skills. A curious mind is a mind that's always growin'.

Day 215 of 365: August 4th

Strength isn't just about physical power; it's about mental resilience to push through the toughest challenges and rise up like a King.

Day 216 of 365: August 5th

Never underestimate the power of knowledge. Educate yourself, read books, seek mentors who have walked the path you aspire to. Knowledge is the key to unlocking doors.

Day 217 of 365: August 6th

Dream big bro. Your imagination knows no bounds. Let your dreams guide you, fuel your passion, and propel you towards greatness. Don't let anyone tell you what you can or can't achieve.

Day 218 of 365: August 7th

t's all about respect, fam. Treat others with respect, show love to your people, and uplift those around you. Remember, real strength lies in building bridges, not tearing them down. But don't let nobody play in your face.

Day 219 of 365: August 8th

But remember, success ain't just about the bread and women. It's about leaving a legacy, changing the game. Lift up your hood, lend a helping hand. Empower those around you, be the leader that you always needed.

Day 220 of 365: August 9th

So, young homies, stand tall, be proud of who you are. Embrace the power within, you're a shining star. The streets may be rough, but you've got what it takes. Your journey awaits, young king, never take your foot off the brakes.

Day 221 of 365: August 10th

Remember, it's not just about the hustle and grind, Take care of your mental, find peace in your mind.

Day 222 of 365: August 11th

We all face hard times, doubts, and fears, it's part of the journey. Don't be afraid to lean on your loved ones, open up to your lady, or even seek professional help if needed. Real strength lies in acknowledging when you need support.

Day 223 of 365: August 12th

Your mental and physical well-being matter. Find time to recharge, to reflect, and to do the things that bring you joy. You deserve it, and you owe it to yourself.

Day 224 of 365: August 13th

Don't let nobody hold you back. You're destined for greatness, and don't you forget it. Surround yourself with positive vibes and people who uplift you. You're the captain of your own ship, so set sail towards your dreams and don't let anyone or anything sink your spirit.

Day 225 of 365: August 14th

Surround yourself with positive vibes and real homies who uplift you. Stay focused on your goals and don't let distractions steer you off track. Keep your head up, stay true to yourself, and stay hungry for success.

Day 226 of 365: August 15th

Remember, it's okay to stumble along the way. Failure is just a temporary setback, not a life sentence. Get back up, learn from your mistakes, and keep moving forward.

Day 227 of 365: August 16th

Real talk, the hardest thing is who to decide to be patient with and who needs to cut off. Can't let people play in your face because you got love for them.

Day 228 of 365: August 17th

It's normal to experience setbacks and disappointments. Allow yourself to process these feelings, but don't let them define you.

Day 229 of 365: August 18th

It's okay to grow and not want to be around the same old, same old. If you keep doing what you've always done, you'll continue to get what you always got. Real talk.

Day 230 of 365: August 19th

Hey bro, don't forget to take care of yourself along the way. Self-care ain't just for the ladies. Make sure you recharge, reflect, and keep your mental and physical well-being in check."

Day 231 of 365: August 20th

Keep that hustle strong! Success ain't handed out for free. Put in the work, grind when nobody's watching, and stay persistent. The hustle pays off.

Day 232 of 365: August 21st

"Listen up, bro! It's time to elevate your game. Don't be afraid to step out of your comfort zone and challenge yourself. Growth happens when you push your limits!

Day 233 of 365: August 22nd

Failure is just feedback, not the end of the road. Learn from your mistakes, adjust your approach, and keep pushing forward. Success is built on the lessons learned from failures."

Day 234 of 365: August 23rd

What's good, bro? Remember, self-improvement isn't just about physical gains or material success. It's also about nurturing your mind, soul, and relationships. Take time for self-care, chase your passions, and foster meaningful connections along the way.

Day 235 of 365: August 24th

You fightin' or you foldin'?

Day 236 of 365: August 25th

Behind every strong g man, there is a story that gave him no choice. Respect!

Day 237 of 365: August 26th

A lot of people saying they wouldn't do what you did, couldn't do what you did. Remember that!

Day 238 of 365: August 27th

Acting out of emotion is going to cost you everything, every time!

Day 239 of 365: August 28th

Just because you grew up that way doesn't mean you have to stay that way. That can't be your excuse.

Day 240 of 365: August 29th

Everything won't always be everything but you still have to do your thing. Can't let up!

I'm proud of you for taking the initiative to better yourself. Navigating life isn't easy, but the fact that you're putting in the effort shows your strength and determination. Keep pushing forward.

Day 241 of 365: August 30th

"Stay hungry, stay humble, and stay teachable, my guy. Be open to learning new things, seeking knowledge, and evolving as a man.

Day 242 of 365: August 31th

Now, we all gonna face setbacks and failures along the way. It's part of the game. But don't let 'em knock you down. Embrace that, bounce back stronger, and learn from those experiences. You got this, big homie.

September : Month of Strengths & Resilience

_____

Day 243 of 365: September 1st

Remember that failure is not the end; it's an opportunity to learn, adapt, and come back stronger than ever before.

Day 244 of 365: September 2nd

Stay grinding and hustling, because success ain't waiting' around for nobody.

Day 245 of 365: September 3rd

Success isn't about luck, it's about hustle. Stay focused, put in the work, and claim what's rightfully yours.

Day 246 of 365: September 4th

Your dreams aren't confined to the block, bro. It's a whole world out there ready for you.

Day 247 of 365: September 5th

Life's a ride, homie. Strap in, enjoy the journey, and create your own path to greatness.

Day 248 of 365: September 6th

Let your struggles be the stepping stones to your success. You're stronger than you know.

Day 249 of 365: September 7th

Strength doesn't come from what you can do; it comes from overcoming what you thought you couldn't.

Day 250 of 365: September 8th

The only person who can limit your potential is you. Break those barriers with discipline and determination.

Day 251 of 365: September 9th

Dream big. No matter where you come from or what challenges you face, dream big, homie. Your ambitions have no limits. Believe in yourself, set those goals, and grind hard to make 'em a reality.

Day 252 of 365: September 10th

You're not defined by your circumstances; you're defined by your response to them. That's true strength.

Day 253 of 365: September 11th

You've been silently winning battles and transforming yourself, be proud of every step you're making in the right direction.

Day 254 of 365: September 12th

Remember, success isn't just about wealth and material possessions. It's about impacting lives, leaving a positive legacy, and lifting others up along the way. Be the change you want to see.

Day 255 of 365: September 13th

Listen more than you Speak. You learn more when you just observe and listen. Become an active listener. Only speak when you have something meaningful to say. Don't be known for the man that has a lot to say but does nothing.

Day 256 of 365: September 14th

It's not about where you come from; it's about where you're going. Your background doesn't' define you —it's your hustle, determination, and ambition that's gonna take you places.

Day 257 of 365: September 15th

We ain't waiting for luck to knock on our door. We're gonna create our own luck, put in that work, and make our dreams happen.

Day 258 of 365: September 16th

Ain't no time for playing small, homies. You gotta dream big and chase after those goals with all you got. It may seem impossible at times, but remember, every great win started with a vision and the belief that it could be done.

Day 259 of 365: September 17th

Real talk, believe in yourself: You got dreams? You got goals? Then believe in yourself like nobody else can. Don't let doubt or negativity hold you back. Trust your instincts, put in the work.

Day 260 of 365: September 18th

Level up, no limits: Don't let anyone put a cap on your potential. Break free from the limits and expectations that society may try to impose on you. Level up your game, aim higher, and push beyond what anyone thought possible.

Day 261 of 365: September 19th

Learn from your Ls: We all take some losses along the way, but it's how you bounce back that matters. Embrace those losses as lessons and use them to grow stronger.

Day 262 of 365: September 20th

Surround yourself with winners: You know what they say, "Show me your crew, and I'll show you your future."

Day 263 of 365: September 21st

In a world that tries to mold you into something you're not, stay true to who you are.

Day 264 of 365: September 22nd

No matter where you come from or what you've been through, you have the power to rise above and create a future that you once only dreamed about.

Day 265 of 365: September 23rd

Ain't no shame in asking for help, fam. We all need a helping hand sometimes. Whether it's seeking advice, learning new skills, or finding a mentor who's been in your shoes, reaching out for support is a sign of strength. Don't let pride hold you back—wise men know when to seek guidance.

Day 266 of 365: September 24th

"Listen, life's a battlefield, and you're the soldier. Embrace the struggle, cause it's gonna mold you into a stronger man. Believe in yourself, trust your instincts, and keep pushing forward. You got this!

Day 267 of 365: September 25th

I know sometimes it feels like the whole world is against you.. Keep your head high, hustle hard, and prove 'em wrong. Success is the sweetest revenge!

Day 268 of 365: September 26th

Embrace the grind, because greatness isn't handed out for free. You have to earn your stripes and pay the price.

Day 269 of 365: September 27th

You got the power within you to overcome anything. You just have to believe it and move like you got something to lose.

Day 270 of 365: September 28TH

Forgive yourself for the choices you made when you didn't know better. Move on. Do better.

Day 271 of 365: September 29th

Practice being calm when you feel like you're being challenged or tested. Don't give your power away for someone to use against you later.

Day 272 of 365: September 30th

You have to trust your gut when it comes to choosing the women you deal with and the homies you surround yourself with. Don't go against yourself.

October: Month of No Turning Back & Pushing Through
_____

Day 273 of 365: October 1ˢᵗ

"Listen up, bros! It's time to step up our game and strive for greatness. Don't settle for mediocrity. Embrace challenges, learn from your mistakes, and never stop grinding.

Day 274 of 365: October 2nd

Don't trip over the haters, they just mad you're walking tall in your own lane.

Day 275 of 365: October 3th

Your worst days are setting you up for your best days, you just have to get through the day.

Day 276 of 365: October 4th

Life's a marathon, so lace up your sneakers and keep running towards your dreams, no matter how far the finish line seems.

Day 277 of 365: October 5th

"Every setback is just a setup for a major comeback. Stay focused and bounce back stronger, my G.

Day 278 of 365: October 6th

Rise above the noise, stay focused on your goals, and let your success make the loudest noise.

Day 279 of 365: October 7th

When life knocks you down, remember you ain't built to break. Rise up, gather your strength, and show 'em what you're made of.

Day 280 of 365: October 8th

Inspiration is all around, hidden in the streets, waiting for those with open eyes and hungry hearts to turn it into something extraordinary.

Day 281 of 365: October 9th

Struggles and obstacles are just tests. Keep pushing', keep fighting, and never fold. Chin up. Chest out. Faith strong.

Day 282 of 365: October 10th

"Life's a puzzle, and you got all the pieces. It's up to you to put 'em together and create a masterpiece,

Day 283 of 365: October 11ᵗʰ

There are no limits to what you can achieve, fam. Break those barriers, chase your goals, and let 'em know you ain't playing.

Day 284 of 365: October 12th

Pay attention to how people treat you when you're up. But more importantly, pay attention to how people treat you when you're down.

Day 285 of 365: October 13th

Don't chase the bag; build an empire and let the bag chase you.

Day 286 of 365: October 14th

In this life, regrets come from turning back, not from pushing forward. Stay focused on your path, stay true to yourself, and never let anything make you turn back."

Day 287 of 365: October 15th

"Life ain't easy, and it ain't meant to be. But you know what? Real men don't back down when things get tough. We stand tall, ten toes down, and keep pushing through.

Day 288 of 365: October 16th

Turning back might seem like the easy way out, but it ain't what you really want to do. Never circle back on things or people that tried to break you.

Day 289 of 365: October 17th

At some point, you gotta help you, save you, change you. The truth is...no one is coming to save you. It's on you.

Day 290 of 365: October 18th

That new life you want so bad is going to require you to let go of the old one completely, no middle ground.

Day 291 of 365: October 19th

Just be real, it saves everyone's time.

Day 292 of 365: October 20ᵗʰ

Missing out on women and temporary fun to build permanent stability is not lame, lock in. You'll thank yourself later.

Day 293 of 365: October 21ˢᵗ

Get up in the morning and go hard for YOU! Stop worrying about what everybody else got going on. You got your own motion. This life is yours to live.

Day 294 of 365: October 22nd

There is no one who can give you what you want better than you can give yourself what you want.

Go HARD!

Day 295 of 365: October 23rd

Learn the difference between the sound of your intuition guiding you and your bad experiences misleading you.

Day 296 of 365: October 24th

Discipline is a form of self-love.

Day 297 of 365: October 25th

Keep the ones who heard you when you never said a word. Cut ties with the rest of them.

Day 298 of 365: October 26th

If something feels off about a person/place/thing it's because something is off. Don't stick around to discover what it is. It'll cost you later.

Day 299 of 365: October 27th

That ugly part of your story that you're living through right now is one of the most significant parts of your life. Push through.

Day 300 of 365: October 28th

To find peace, you have to be willing to lose your connection with the people, places, and things that create the noise. Take accountability for your part and adjust as necessary.

Day 301 of 365: October 29th

The man you will be in 5 years depends largely on what and who you are entertaining in this current moment.

Day 303 of 365: October 30th

Sometimes you have all the support in the world and sometimes it's just you. Be willing to handle the times when no one is clapping for you.

Day 304 of 365: October 31st

You gotta be careful who you put first, you may be last to them.

November: Month of Realizing Your Power & Greatness

_____

Day 305 of 365: November 1st

Elevate your mind, my man. Keep learning, growing, and expanding your knowledge. Read books, listen to podcasts, engage in meaningful conversations. The more you know, the more powerful you become.

Day 306 of 365: November 2nd

Stay woke, homie. Be aware of what's happening around you. Stay informed, educated, and engaged. Knowledge is power, and it'll help you navigate this crazy world.

Day 307 of 365: November 3rd

"Stay true to yourself and hustle hard. There are no limits to what you can achieve, fam.

Day 308 of 365: November 4th

Don't be afraid to take risks, bro. If you keep doing what you've always done, you'll continue to get what you always got.

Day 309 of 365: November 5th

Remember, fam, your past doesn't define your future. Rise above your circumstances and create a legacy that inspires others.

Day 310 of 365: November 6th

No matter where you come from, it's where you're headed those matters. Aim high and make it happen.

Day 311 of 365: November 7th

Yea bro, the struggle is real, but so is your hustle. Keep pushing, keep hustling, and watch things change. Slow progress is still progress. Remember that.

Day 312 of 365: November 8th

Don't let the past define you, homie. It's all about the future you create and the choices you make.

Day 313 of 365: November 10

Never forget your worth, young king. You are capable of greatness. Believe in yourself, chase your dreams, and never let anyone tell you otherwise. You got the power within you to make a difference and leave a legacy.

Day 314 of 365: November 11

Yo, fam, remember this: stars can't shine without darkness. Embrace the struggle, cause it's just a chapter in your success story. Keep grinding and watch how you light the sky.

Day 315 of 365: November 12

You ain't missing out on nothing when you're trying to get your sh*t together. As a man, you can't be out here with nothing. Stay focused and build something you can be proud of. All the other stuff will be there when you're done.

Day 316 of 365: November 13th

Even if you hit rock bottom and have no idea what's next, never go back to anything/anyone that tried to break you.

Day 317 of 365: November 14th

Learn when to speak, when to listen, and when to just leave. Your life can depend on it.

Day 318 of 365: November 15th

You can't expect to be great at what you do if you're not willing to keep going when times get tough. Believe me, times will get tough.

Day 319 of 365: November 16th

……We don't give up around here.

November 17th

You didn't make it this far to make it this far. There's more work to be done. Your current situation isn't your final destination.

November 18th

People will quit on you. Women will leave you. Homies will switch up on you. That's life, but never give up on yourself.

November 19th

In a blink of an eye, you can be down just as quick as you were up. Stay humble.

November 20th

Force yourself to get up early. Take care of your responsibilities. Be honest with yourself and evaluate your priorities and handle your business.

November 21st

Don't fall back into your old patterns because they are familiar.

November 22nd

Everybody did what was best for them. Your turn.

November 23rd

Sometimes you're not even mad at the person, you just thought they were realer than that and hate you gave them the benefit of the doubt.

November 24th

If you don't heal what hurt you, you'll bleed on people who didn't cut you.

November 25th

It's about EFFORT. As a man, you'll ever be perfect but when you bring that effort every single day, that's when things change.

November 26th

Don't let another man speak limitations over your life. What he couldn't do has nothing to do with you.

November 27th

Accept people as they are but place people where they belong.

November 28

You have to decide what's important to you and choose what matters most.

November 29th

When life knocks you down, make sure you land on your feet and bounce back harder. Life is like a marathon, and you're built for endurance. Pace yourself, stay determined, and cross that finish line. Just keep going!

November 30th

Don't wait for opportunity to knock. Kick the door down and make it happen. If you don't work, you won't eat. No one owes you nothing.

December: Month of Reflection & Redirection

_____

December 1st

Stay hungry, stay humble. Never forget where you came from while chasing your dreams.

December 2nd

You can't soar with eagles if you're hanging with pigeons. Surround yourself with winners and elevate. Eventually every man will show you his true face.

December 3rd

There's no shortcuts to greatness; you gotta put in the work to reach the top. Trying to cut corners will keep you where you are.

December 4th

"Don't let the noise of the streets drown out the beat of your heart. Let it guide you to your dreams.

December 5th

Remember, it's all about the hustle and the grind. Stay focused on your goals, put in the work, and don't be afraid to get your hands dirty. Success doesn't come easy, but you know what they say: "No pain, no gain." Keep pushing, stay motivated, and trust in your ability to overcome any setback that comes.

December 6th

The streets might be rough, but your spirit is tougher. Embrace the challenges and let 'em fuel your hunger for success.

December 7th

Life's a journey, fam, so stay woke, stay focused, and make sure your hustle matches your hunger.

December 8th

Success really ain't for the weak. It takes discipline, determination, and a whole lot of hustle.

December 9th

Don't be afraid to say NO to opportunities that don't quite align with the man you're trying to become.

December 10th

Keep your head up, eyes on the prize. There's nothing you can't handle, you a straight-up boss.

December 11th

Lift yourself up, no matter how deep you've fallen. Bounce back like a real G and keep it moving.

December 12th

Remember, young kings, you have the power within you to overcome any challenge, to rise above any circumstance. Believe in yourself, stay true to your values, and keep grindin'.

December 13th

Dream Bigger, Aim Higher. Don't limit yourself, my man. Dream big, envision your goals, and then go after them like a boss. Don't let anyone tell you what you can or can't achieve. Set your sights high and keep pushing until you reach those dreams.

December 14th

Aye, I know the struggle's real, but remember, you're a warrior, not a worrier. Keep fighting, keep pushing, and watch how you bounce back stronger.

December 15th

"I feel you, fam. Life's throwing punches, but you're built to take 'em. Dust yourself off, get back up, and keep fighting. You're a champion in the making.

December 16th

Keep your head up, even when life's got you feeling down. The only way to get through the darkest days is to remember that only the strong will survive mentally, physically, and emotionally. Feel what you need to feel but you just can't walk in defeat.

December 17th

Yo, don't let them struggles define you, homie. Rise above the hate, flex that strength, and prove 'em wrong. Your comeback going to make everybody regret doubting you.

December 18th

Ain't no time for excuses, fam. Time to man up and make things happen. Believe in yourself and watch how it all plays out.

December 19th

Yo, haters gonna hate, but don't let 'em bring you down. Rise above the negativity and drown out the noise. Don't let anything distract you from walking in your purpose and becoming the man you're meant to be.

December 20th

Stop self-sabotaging because you are afraid of failing. So what, you may not get it right the first time. The second time around, you move from experience, you're no longer a beginner.

December 21st

Who you are experiencing life with in the moment is more important than ever. Look around. Look at your circle. Look at the woman/women you're dealing with. Access. Do what needs to be done.

December 22nd

Note to Self: Don't settle for mid. Being love is the minimum. Make sure you are also respected.

December 23rd

One day you'll look back on your life and understand the well-intentioned version of yourself back then that didn't always get things right.

December 24th

The game of life ain't fair, but that's just fuel for your fire. Embrace the struggle and make your comeback legendary.

December 25th

"In a world where the odds are stacked against us, strength is the armor we wear to fight our battles.

December 26th

Your time is limited, so don't waste it living someone else's life. Man up and to follow your own path.

December 27th

Strength doesn't come from what you can do. It comes from overcoming the things you once thought you couldn't."

December 28th

Life's a journey, fam, so stay woke, stay focused, and make sure your hustle matches your hunger."

December 29th

No matter where you start, it's about how you rise. Turn your struggle into your strength.

December 30th

You're the author of your own story, fam. So make it a bestseller, flipping every page with determination and purpose.

December 31st

Overall, stay true to yourself, stay loyal, stay humble, work hard, help others, protect your peace, and find happiness in little things. You only get one life to live.

Made in the USA
Columbia, SC
03 July 2023